NICOTEXT

the guide to doing me

DO NOT DRINK AND DRIVE & DO NOT DRINK ALCOHOL
IF YOU ARE UNDER DRINKING AGE!

...AND KIDS, REMEMBER, ALWAYS WEAR A CONDOM!

Copyright ©NICOTEXT 2008 All rights reserved.
NICOTEXT part of Cladd media ltd.
ISBN: 978-91-85869-28-2
Printed in Poland

HELLO, THIS IS ME

MY NAME IS:

....

....

MY AGE:

....

I WORK WITH:

....

....

....

SINGLE /MARRIED/ ATTACHED:

....

AGES OF SIGNIFICANCE

AGES OF SIGNIFICANCE

MY FIRST KISS:..

THE FIRST TIME I MASTURBATED:.............
....

THE VERY FIRST TIME I ASKED SOME-ONE TO BE MY GIRL- /BOYFRIEND/ MY FIRST PUPPY-LOVE:.............................
....

THE FIRST TIME I TRIED PETTING:...........
....

THE FIRST TIME I HAD SEX:.....................
....

THE FIRST TIME I HAD AN ORGASM: ....

THE FIRST TIME I FLIRTED: ....

THE FIRST TIME I HAD ORAL SEX: ....

THE FIRST TIME I SAW A PORNO MOVIE/ LOOKED IN A DIRTY MAGAZINE:

FILL IN THE BLANKS

THE NAME OF MY FIRST BOYFRIEND/
GIRLFRIEND WAS ....

THE NAME OF THE FIRST PERSON I
KISSED WAS..
I LOST MY VIRGINITY IN..
....................................WITH....................................

THREE WORDS TO DESCRIBE THE FIRST
TIME ARE..

....

A SEXUAL EXPERIMENT I DID WHEN I WAS
YOUNG..

....

....

I FIRST RECEIVED ORAL SEX.............................

AND IT HAPPENED WITH....................................
....
....THE BIGGEST AGE
DIFFERENCE BETWEEN ME AND A SEX
PARTNER IS...YEARS
THE WORST SEX I EVER HAD WAS.............

....

...........THE WEIRDEST SEXUAL REQUEST
SOMEONE HAS ASKED ME TO PERFORM

....

....

THE WEIRDEST PLACE I'VE HAD SEX IS

....

....

FILL IN THE BLANKS

MY MOST EMBARRASSING SEX MOMENT

....

....

A SEXUAL ACT I'VE TRIED ONCE AND WILL NEVER TRY AGAIN...................

....

SOMETHING I WOULD NEVER CONSIDER DOING IS..

....

....

....

.... THE LONGEST PERIOD OF TIME I'VE GONE WITHOUT SEX...................

....

NUMBERS

NUMBER OF SEXUAL PARTNERS:
NONE   1-5   5-10   10-20
20-40   40+   I DON'T KNOW

NUMBER OF ONE-NIGHT-STANDS:
NONE   1-5   5-10   10-20
20-40   40+   I DON'T KNOW

NUMBER OF TIMES I'VE HAD SEX IN THE LAST 90 DAYS:
NONE   1-5   5-10   10-20
20-40   40+   I DON'T KNOW

NUMBER OF SERIOUS RELATIONSHIPS:
NONE   1-5   5-10   10-20
20-40   40+   I DON'T KNOW

NUMBER OF TIMES I'VE MASTURBATED
IN THE LAST MONTH:
NONE   1-5   5-10   10-20
20-40   40+   I DON'T KNOW

YES/NO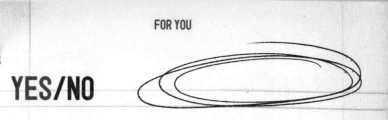

I HAVE ALWAYS BEEN SURE OF
MY SEXUAL DISPOSITION.
YES/NO

I HAVE HAD A STD (SEXUALLY
TRANSMITTED DISEASE).
YES/NO

I'M STILL IN TOUCH WITH THE
PERSON I LOST MY VIRGINITY TO.
YES/NO

I HAVE MADE PORN WITH A
SEXUAL PARTNER.
YES/NO

YES/NO

I'VE WATCHED PORN WITH A
SEXUAL PARTNER.
YES/NO

I'VE CHEATED ON SOMEONE.
YES/NO

I'VE HAD SEX IN A PUBLIC PLACE.
YES/NO

I'VE HAD GROUP SEX.
YES/NO

YES/NO

I'VE HAD ANAL SEX.
YES/NO

I'VE MASTURBATED AT MY
WORK PLACE.
YES/NO

I'VE MASTURBATED AT MY SCHOOL.
YES/NO

I'VE HAD SADOSEX.
YES/NO

YES/NO

I'VE TRIED SEXUAL ROLE PLAY.
YES/NO

I'VE MASTURBATED IN FRONT
OF A MIRROR.
YES/NO

I'VE BEEN CAUGHT MASTURBATING.
YES/NO

I'VE HAD SEX WITH SOMEONE OUT
OF PITY.
YES/NO

YES/NO

I'VE BEEN CAUGHT IN THE ACT.
YES/NO

I'VE CAUGHT SOMEONE ELSE HAVING SEX.
YES/NO

I'VE BEEN TO A STRIP CLUB.
YES/NO

I'VE PAID SOMEONE MONEY FOR SEX.
YES/NO

YES/NO

I'VE ACCEPTED MONEY FOR SEX.
YES/NO

I'VE HAD SEX WITH A BOSS.
YES/NO

I'VE HAD SEX WITH ONE OF MY
EMPLOYEES.
YES/NO

I'VE HAD SEX WITH ONE OF MY
TEACHERS OR PROFESSORS.
YES/NO

YES/NO

I'VE HAD SEX WITH SOMEONE I
WAS TEACHING.
YES/NO

I'VE HAD SEX WITH SOMEONE FROM MY
CHURCH/TEMPLE.
YES/NO

I'VE HAD SEX WHILE VERY
INTOXICATED.
YES/NO

I'VE HAD SEX WITH SOMEONE WHO WAS
VERY INTOXICATED.
YES/NO

YES/NO

I'VE HAD SEX WITH SOMEONE OF
THE SAME SEX.
YES/NO

I'VE HAD SEX WITH SOMEONE OF THE
OPPOSITE SEX.
YES/NO

I'VE HAD SEX WITH MORE THAN ONE
PERSON AT A TIME.
YES/NO

I'VE HAD SEX WHEN I KNEW OTHER
PEOPLE WERE WATCHING.
YES/NO

ONE TIME I HAD SEX WITH
MORE THAN ONE PERSON
IN A DAY.

YES/NO

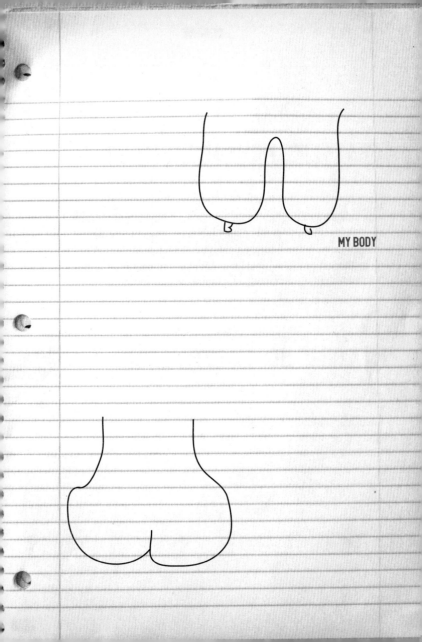

MY BODY

WHAT I LIKE MOST ABOUT MY BODY:

1...

2...

3...

MY THREE MOST EROTIC SPOTS:

1...

2...

3...

MY PARTS

DRAW A LINE

SENSITIVE   TICKLISH   FORBIDDEN

TENDER

INSENSITIVE

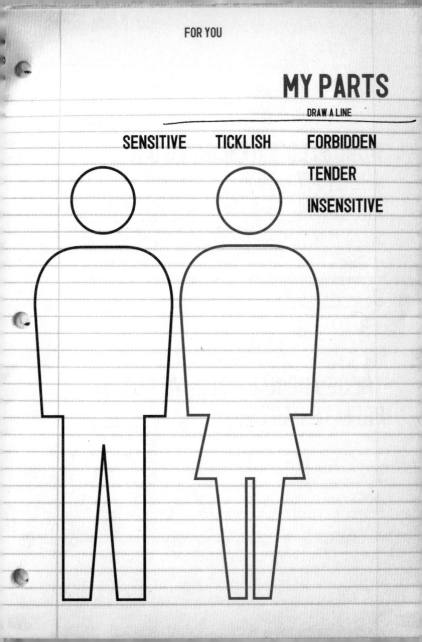

WORDS I LIKE OTHERS TO USE ABOUT MY BODY:

1..
2..
3..

THESE ARE NAMES I HAVE FOR MY PRIVATE PARTS:

1..
2..
3..

MY TURN ONS (AND TURN OFFS)

MY TURN ONS (AND TURN OFFS)

WHAT IS THE FIRST THING YOU NOTICE ABOUT SOMEONE YOU ARE ATTRACTED TO?

....

....

....

SECOND THING?

....

....

....

THIRD THING?

....

....

....

....

....

FIVE BODY PARTS THAT TURN ME ON THE MOST:

EYES

HAIR

ARMS

HANDS

ASS

FEET

TOES

CHIN

LIPS

BREASTS/CHEST

BACK

EARS

NOSE

MOUTH

FINGERS

STOMACH/BELLY

SHOULDERS

FACE

LEGS

INNER THIGH

NECK

OTHER:

MY FANTASIES

I HAVE AT SOME POINT FANTASIZED ABOUT:

- ☐ SPANKING
- ☐ GROUP SEX
- ☐ HAVING SEX WHILE SOMEONE ELSE IS WATCHING
- ☐ BEING PHYSICALLY RESTRAINED DURING A SEXUAL SCENARIO
- ☐ BDSM
- ☐ HAVING SEX WITH SOMEONE OF THE SAME SEX
- ☐ A GOLDEN SHOWER

THIS TURNS ME OFF:

1. ....

2. ....

3. ....

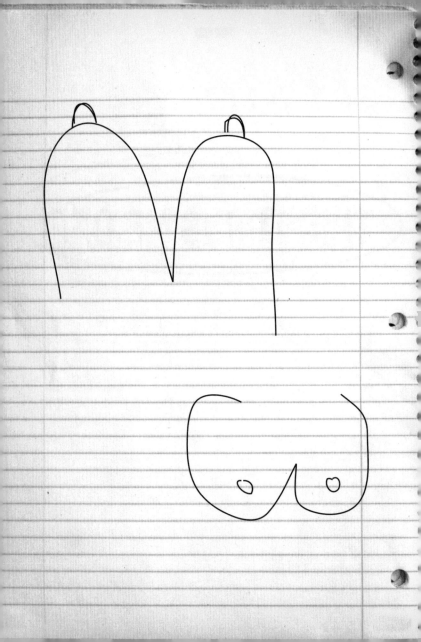

FOREPLAY

WHEN WE ARE KISSING I LIKE:

☐ TO MAKE THE FIRST MOVE

☐ TO KISS ON THE LIPS WITH NO TONGUE

☐ TO KISS WITH A LOT OF TONGUE

☐ TO KISS WITH MOUTH WIDE OPEN

☐ TO KISS WITH MY MOUTH A LITTLE TIGHT

☐ TO KEEP MY EYES CLOSED

PLEASE DO NOT EAT THE FOLLOWING THINGS BEFORE WE KISS: (AND I WON'T EITHER!)

....

....

DIRTY TALK

I LIKE DIRTY TALK. YES/NO

I LIKE HEARING YOU TELLING ME ABOUT..............
....**I WANT YOU**
TO SAY..
.........**AND TELL ME**...
....**WHEN YOU**..............................
....**I LIKE FOR OUR DIRTY**
TALK TO INCLUDE WORDS LIKE..

....

...............................**AND**...
.................................**TELL ME HOW YOU**..............................
....**IN DETAIL.**
I LIKE IT WHEN YOU'RE TALKING DIRTY
BECAUSE...

DURING FOREPLAY I LIKE IT WHEN YOU STIMULATE ME WITH THE HELP OF

MOUTH
1 - 2 - 3 - 4 - 5
HANDS AND FINGERS
1 - 2 - 3 - 4 - 5
SEX TOYS
1 - 2 - 3 - 4 - 5
FEATHERS
1 - 2 - 3 - 4 - 5
FOOD
1 - 2 - 3 - 4 - 5
ICE
1 - 2 - 3 - 4 - 5

FILL IN THE BLANKS

IT MAKES ME FEEL _____ WHEN
YOU _____.

WHEN WE'RE KISSING I LIKE TO PUT
MY HANDS _____ AND
_____ OR _____.

I LOVE THE WAY YOU

_____

FILL IN THE BLANKS

I LIKE YOU TO PUT YOUR
HANDS_____
AND_____ OR
_____

REMEMBER THAT THING YOU DID
WHEN_____? DO IT AGAIN,
BUT_____!

YOU'RE SO GOOD AT
_____!

THE INTERCOURSE

MY FAVORITE PLACES TO HAVE **SEX:**

1...

2...

3...

THIS IS HOW MUCH I ENJOY

MORNING SEX
1 - 2 - 3 - 4 - 5

BOOTY CALL SEX
1 - 2 - 3 - 4 - 5

QUICKIE
1 - 2 - 3 - 4 - 5

DRUNKEN SEX
1 - 2 - 3 - 4 - 5

ONE NIGHT STANDS
1 - 2 - 3 - 4 - 5

THIS IS THE NORMAL AMOUNT FOR US TO HAVE SEX, IN MY OPINION:

MUSIC I LIKE HAVING SEX TO:

TOUCH ME HERE!

DRAW A LINE

KISS
CARESS
MASSAGE
TOUCH
TICKLE
BRUSH
RUB
EMBRACE
LICK
BLOW
PINCH

POSITIONS

THESE ARE THE POSITIONS I'VE TRIED. I'M RATING EACH ONE FROM 1-5. 1 MEANING I WOULD RATHER POKE A STICK IN MY EYE THAN DO IT AGAIN AND 5 MEANING I COULD DO THIS AT BREAKFAST, LUNCH, AND DINNER

ME ON TOP
1 - 2 - 3 - 4 - 5

ME ON BOTTOM
1 - 2 - 3 - 4 - 5

FROM BEHIND (KNEELING)
1 - 2 - 3 - 4 - 5

FROM BEHIND (LYING DOWN)
1 - 2 - 3 - 4 - 5

SIXTY-NINE
1 - 2 - 3 - 4 - 5

STANDING UP
1 - 2 - 3 - 4 - 5

WHILE STANDING ON MY HEAD
1 - 2 - 3 - 4 - 5
WHILE THE OTHER PERSON STANDS ON HIS/
HER HEAD
1 - 2 - 3 - 4 - 5
PERSON ON BOTTOM SITTING UP
1 - 2 - 3 - 4 - 5
LEGS BEHIND MY HEAD
1 - 2 - 3 - 4 - 5
WITH PARTNER'S LEGS BEHIND HIS/
HER HEAD
1 - 2 - 3 - 4 - 5
STANDING ON ONE FOOT
1 - 2 - 3 - 4 - 5

LIKES/DISLIKES

I LIKE TO MOAN
1 - 2 - 3 - 4 - 5
I LIKE HEARING MY PARTNER MOAN
1 - 2 - 3 - 4 - 5
I LIKE TO PLAY WITH MYSELF
DURING THE ACT
1 - 2 - 3 - 4 - 5
I LIKE RECEIVING ORAL SEX
1 - 2 - 3 - 4 - 5
I LIKE GIVING ORAL SEX
1 - 2 - 3 - 4 - 5
I LIKE SENSUAL SEX
1 - 2 - 3 - 4 - 5
I LIKE IT ROUGH
1 - 2 - 3 - 4 - 5

I LIKE HEARING DIRTY TALK
1 - 2 - 3 - 4 - 5
I LIKE TALKING DIRTY
1 - 2 - 3 - 4 - 5
I LIKE IT KINKY
1 - 2 - 3 - 4 - 5
I LIKE WATCHING PORN WHILE I'M
HAVING SEX
1 - 2 - 3 - 4 - 5
I LIKE SWALLOWING / I LIKE IT WHEN
YOU SWALLOW
1 - 2 - 3 - 4 - 5
I LIKE HAVING THE LIGHTS ON
1 - 2 - 3 - 4 - 5
I THINK SIZE MATTERS
1 - 2 - 3 - 4 - 5

FANTASIES 1-10

THIS IS MY FANTASY CHECKLIST. I WILL CHECK THEM OFF AFTER
FULFILLING THEM:

1.

2.

3.

4.

5.

6.

7.

8,

9.

10.

IF I WAS TO CHOOSE ONLY ONE SEX
POSITION I WOULD HAVE TO PUT UP
WITH MY WHOLE LIFE, IT WOULD BE:

THIS IS THE NUMBER OF POSITIONS I LIKE
TO HAVE DURING THE ACT:

DIRTY WORDS

THESE ARE MY TOP DIRTY WORDS:

1.

2.

3.

4.

5.

6.

7.

8.

9.

10.

FILL IN THE BLANKS

THE WORST THING YOU CAN DO DURING
SEX IS TO_____

THE WORST THING YOU CAN SAY DURING
SEX IS_____.

SOME TIME I WOULD LIKE FOR US TO
TRY _____

_____.

I USUALLY_____
AFTER SEX

FOR YOUR PARTNER
TO ANSWER

HELLO, THIS IS ME

MY NAME IS:

....

....

MY AGE:

....

I WORK WITH:

....

....

....

SINGLE /MARRIED/ ATTACHED:

....

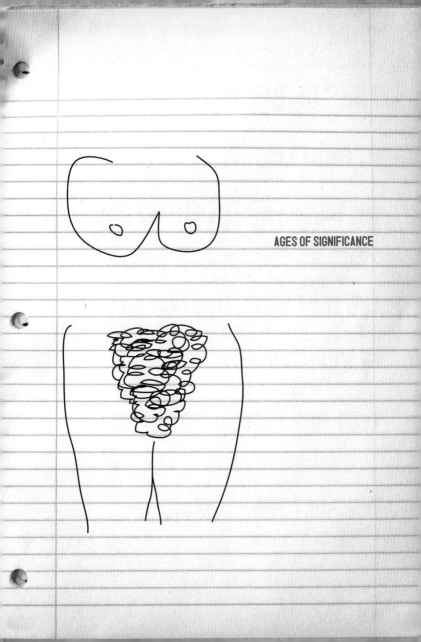

AGES OF SIGNIFICANCE

AGES OF SIGNIFICANCE

MY FIRST KISS:

THE FIRST TIME I MASTURBATED:

THE VERY FIRST TIME I ASKED SOMEONE TO BE MY GIRL- /BOYFRIEND/ MY FIRST PUPPY-LOVE:

THE FIRST TIME I TRIED PETTING:

THE FIRST TIME I HAD SEX:

THE FIRST TIME I HAD AN ORGASM: ....
....

THE FIRST TIME I FLIRTED: ....
....

THE FIRST TIME I HAD ORAL SEX: ....
....

THE FIRST TIME I SAW A PORNO MOVIE/
LOOKED IN A DIRTY MAGAZINE:

....

FILL IN THE BLANKS

THE NAME OF MY FIRST BOYFRIEND/
GIRLFRIEND WAS ....

....

THE NAME OF THE FIRST PERSON I
KISSED WAS...
I LOST MY VIRGINITY IN.......................................
....WITH...................................

....

THREE WORDS TO DESCRIBE THE FIRST
TIME ARE..

....

....

A SEXUAL EXPERIMENT I DID WHEN I WAS
YOUNG..

....

....

I FIRST RECEIVED ORAL SEX............................

AND IT HAPPENED WITH...............................

....

......................................THE BIGGEST AGE
DIFFERENCE BETWEEN ME AND A SEX
PARTNER IS...YEARS
THE WORST SEX I EVER HAD WAS...............

....

....

............THE WEIRDEST SEXUAL REQUEST
SOMEONE HAS ASKED ME TO PERFORM

....

....

THE WEIRDEST PLACE I'VE HAD SEX IS

....

....

FILL IN THE BLANKS

MY MOST EMBARRASSING SEX MOMENT

....

A SEXUAL ACT I'VE TRIED ONCE AND WILL NEVER TRY AGAIN.................................

....

SOMETHING I WOULD NEVER CONSIDER DOING IS...

....

....

....

...........................THE LONGEST PERIOD OF TIME I'VE GONE WITHOUT SEX.................

....

NUMBERS

NUMBER OF SEXUAL PARTNERS:

NONE   1-5   5-10   10-20
20-40   40+   I DON'T KNOW

NUMBER OF ONE-NIGHT-STANDS:

NONE   1-5   5-10   10-20
20-40   40+   I DON'T KNOW

NUMBER OF TIMES I'VE HAD SEX IN THE LAST 90 DAYS:

NONE   1-5   5-10   10-20
20-40   40+   I DON'T KNOW

NUMBER OF SERIOUS RELATIONSHIPS:
NONE   1-5   5-10   10-20
20-40   40+   I DON'T KNOW

NUMBER OF TIMES I'VE MASTURBATED
IN THE LAST MONTH:
NONE   1-5   5-10   10-20
20-40   40+   I DON'T KNOW

YES/NO

I HAVE ALWAYS BEEN SURE OF
MY SEXUAL DISPOSITION.
YES/NO

I HAVE HAD A STD (SEXUALLY
TRANSMITTED DISEASE).
YES/NO

I'M STILL IN TOUCH WITH THE
PERSON I LOST MY VIRGINITY TO.
YES/NO

I HAVE MADE PORN WITH A
SEXUAL PARTNER.
YES/NO

YES/NO

I'VE WATCHED PORN WITH A
SEXUAL PARTNER.
YES/NO

I'VE CHEATED ON SOMEONE.
YES/NO

I'VE HAD SEX IN A PUBLIC PLACE.
YES/NO

I'VE HAD GROUP SEX.
YES/NO

YES/NO

I'VE HAD ANAL SEX.
YES/NO

I'VE MASTURBATED AT MY
WORK PLACE.
YES/NO

I'VE MASTURBATED AT MY SCHOOL.
YES/NO

I'VE HAD SADOSEX.
YES/NO

YES/NO

I'VE TRIED SEXUAL ROLE PLAY.
YES/NO

I'VE MASTURBATED IN FRONT
OF A MIRROR.
YES/NO

I'VE BEEN CAUGHT MASTURBATING.
YES/NO

I'VE HAD SEX WITH SOMEONE OUT
OF PITY.
YES/NO

YES/NO

I'VE BEEN CAUGHT IN THE ACT.
YES/NO

**I'VE CAUGHT SOMEONE ELSE
HAVING SEX.**
YES/NO

I'VE BEEN TO A STRIP CLUB.
YES/NO

I'VE PAID SOMEONE MONEY FOR SEX.
YES/NO

YES/NO

I'VE ACCEPTED MONEY FOR SEX.
YES/NO

I'VE HAD SEX WITH A BOSS.
YES/NO

I'VE HAD SEX WITH ONE OF MY EMPLOYEES.
YES/NO

I'VE HAD SEX WITH ONE OF MY TEACHERS OR PROFESSORS.
YES/NO

YES/NO

I'VE HAD SEX WITH SOMEONE I
WAS TEACHING.
YES/NO

I'VE HAD SEX WITH SOMEONE FROM MY
CHURCH/TEMPLE.
YES/NO

I'VE HAD SEX WHILE VERY
INTOXICATED.
YES/NO

I'VE HAD SEX WITH SOMEONE WHO WAS
VERY INTOXICATED.
YES/NO

YES/NO

I'VE HAD SEX WITH SOMEONE OF
THE SAME SEX.
YES/NO

I'VE HAD SEX WITH SOMEONE OF THE
OPPOSITE SEX.
YES/NO

I'VE HAD SEX WITH MORE THAN ONE
PERSON AT A TIME.
YES/NO

I'VE HAD SEX WHEN I KNEW OTHER
PEOPLE WERE WATCHING.
YES/NO

ONE TIME I HAD SEX WITH MORE THAN ONE PERSON IN A DAY.

YES/NO

MY BODY

WHAT I LIKE MOST ABOUT MY BODY:

1..

2..

3..

MY THREE MOST EROTIC SPOTS:

1..

2..

3..

MY PARTS

DRAW A LINE

SENSITIVE TICKLISH FORBIDDEN

TENDER

INSENSITIVE

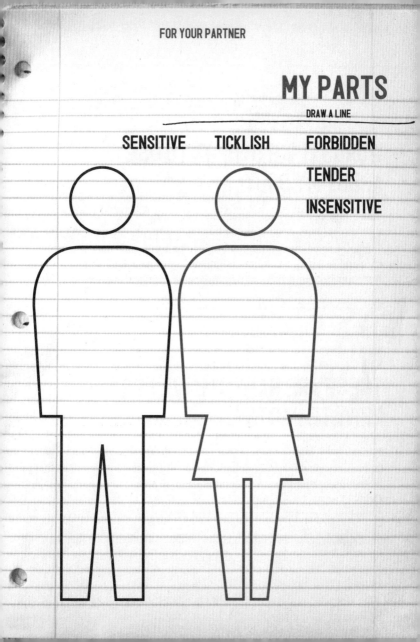

WORDS I LIKE OTHERS TO USE ABOUT MY BODY:

1...
2...
3...

THESE ARE NAMES I HAVE FOR MY PRIVATE PARTS:

1...
2...
3...

MY TURN ONS (AND TURN OFFS)

MY TURN ONS (AND TURN OFFS)

WHAT IS THE FIRST THING YOU NOTICE ABOUT SOMEONE YOU ARE ATTRACTED TO?

....

....

....

SECOND THING?

....

....

....

THIRD THING?

....

....

....

....

....

FIVE BODY PARTS THAT TURN ME ON THE MOST:

EYES
HAIR
ARMS
HANDS
ASS
FEET
TOES
CHIN
LIPS
BREASTS/CHEST
BACK
EARS
NOSE

MOUTH
FINGERS
STOMACH/BELLY
SHOULDERS
FACE
LEGS
INNER THIGH
NECK

OTHER:

MY FANTASIES

I HAVE AT SOME POINT FANTASIZED ABOUT:

- ☐ SPANKING
- ☐ GROUP SEX
- ☐ HAVING SEX WHILE SOMEONE ELSE IS WATCHING
- ☐ BEING PHYSICALLY RESTRAINED DURING A SEXUAL SCENARIO
- ☐ BDSM
- ☐ HAVING SEX WITH SOMEONE OF THE SAME SEX
- ☐ A GOLDEN SHOWER

THIS TURNS ME OFF:

1..

2..

3..

FOREPLAY

WHEN WE ARE KISSING I LIKE:

☐ TO MAKE THE FIRST MOVE
☐ TO KISS ON THE LIPS WITH NO TONGUE
☐ TO KISS WITH A LOT OF TONGUE
☐ TO KISS WITH MOUTH WIDE OPEN
☐ TO KISS WITH MY MOUTH A LITTLE TIGHT
☐ TO KEEP MY EYES CLOSED

PLEASE DO NOT EAT THE FOLLOWING THINGS BEFORE WE KISS: (AND I WON'T EITHER!)

....

....

DIRTY TALK

I LIKE DIRTY TALK. YES/NO

I LIKE HEARING YOU TELLING ME ABOUT.............
....I WANT YOU
TO SAY...
.......AND TELL ME...
...............................WHEN YOU...
.... I LIKE FOR OUR DIRTY
TALK TO INCLUDE WORDS LIKE.....................................

....

.......................AND...
..................TELL ME HOW YOU................................
...............................IN DETAIL.
I LIKE IT WHEN YOU'RE TALKING DIRTY
BECAUSE...

DURING FOREPLAY I LIKE IT WHEN YOU STIMULATE ME WITH THE HELP OF

MOUTH
1 - 2 - 3 - 4 - 5

HANDS AND FINGERS
1 - 2 - 3 - 4 - 5

SEX TOYS
1 - 2 - 3 - 4 - 5

FEATHERS
1 - 2 - 3 - 4 - 5

FOOD
1 - 2 - 3 - 4 - 5

ICE
1 - 2 - 3 - 4 - 5

FILL IN THE BLANKS

IT MAKES ME FEEL _____ WHEN
YOU _____.

WHEN WE'RE KISSING I LIKE TO PUT
MY HANDS _____ AND
_____ OR _____.

I LOVE THE WAY YOU

_____

FILL IN THE BLANKS

I LIKE YOU TO PUT YOUR
HANDS_____
AND_____ OR

_____

REMEMBER THAT THING YOU DID
WHEN_____? DO IT AGAIN,
BUT_____!

YOU'RE SO GOOD AT

_____!

THE INTERCOURSE

MY FAVORITE PLACES TO HAVE SEX:

1..

2..

3..

THIS IS HOW MUCH I ENJOY

MORNING SEX
1 - 2 - 3 - 4 - 5

BOOTY CALL SEX
1 - 2 - 3 - 4 - 5

QUICKIE
1 - 2 - 3 - 4 - 5

DRUNKEN SEX
1 - 2 - 3 - 4 - 5

ONE NIGHT STANDS
1 - 2 - 3 - 4 - 5

THIS IS THE NORMAL AMOUNT FOR US TO HAVE SEX, IN MY OPINION:

MUSIC I LIKE HAVING SEX TO:

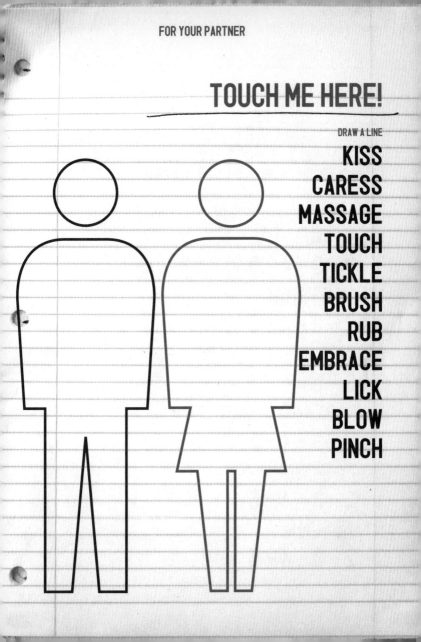

POSITIONS

THESE ARE THE POSITIONS I'VE TRIED. I'M RATING EACH ONE FROM 1-5. 1 MEANING I WOULD RATHER POKE A STICK IN MY EYE THAN DO IT AGAIN AND 5 MEANING I COULD DO THIS AT BREAKFAST, LUNCH, AND DINNER

ME ON TOP
1 - 2 - 3 - 4 - 5

ME ON BOTTOM
1 - 2 - 3 - 4 - 5

FROM BEHIND (KNEELING)
1 - 2 - 3 - 4 - 5

FROM BEHIND (LYING DOWN)
1 - 2 - 3 - 4 - 5

SIXTY-NINE
1 - 2 - 3 - 4 - 5

STANDING UP
1 - 2 - 3 - 4 - 5

WHILE STANDING ON MY HEAD

1 - 2 - 3 - 4 - 5

WHILE THE OTHER PERSON STANDS ON HIS/
HER HEAD

1 - 2 - 3 - 4 - 5

PERSON ON BOTTOM SITTING UP

1 - 2 - 3 - 4 - 5

LEGS BEHIND MY HEAD

1 - 2 - 3 - 4 - 5

WITH PARTNER'S LEGS BEHIND HIS/
HER HEAD

1 - 2 - 3 - 4 - 5

STANDING ON ONE FOOT

1 - 2 - 3 - 4 - 5

LIKES/DISLIKES

I LIKE TO MOAN
1 - 2 - 3 - 4 - 5

I LIKE HEARING MY PARTNER MOAN
1 - 2 - 3 - 4 - 5

I LIKE TO PLAY WITH MYSELF
DURING THE ACT
1 - 2 - 3 - 4 - 5

I LIKE RECEIVING ORAL SEX
1 - 2 - 3 - 4 - 5

I LIKE GIVING ORAL SEX
1 - 2 - 3 - 4 - 5

I LIKE SENSUAL SEX
1 - 2 - 3 - 4 - 5

I LIKE IT ROUGH
1 - 2 - 3 - 4 - 5

I LIKE HEARING DIRTY TALK
1 - 2 - 3 - 4 - 5
I LIKE TALKING DIRTY
1 - 2 - 3 - 4 - 5
I LIKE IT KINKY
1 - 2 - 3 - 4 - 5
I LIKE WATCHING PORN WHILE I'M
HAVING SEX
1 - 2 - 3 - 4 - 5
I LIKE SWALLOWING / I LIKE IT WHEN
YOU SWALLOW
1 - 2 - 3 - 4 - 5
I LIKE HAVING THE LIGHTS ON
1 - 2 - 3 - 4 - 5
I THINK SIZE MATTERS
1 - 2 - 3 - 4 - 5

FANTASIES 1-10

THIS IS MY FANTASY CHECKLIST. I WILL CHECK THEM OFF AFTER FULFILLING THEM:

1.

2.

3.

4.

5.

6.

7.

8,

9.

10.

IF I WAS TO CHOOSE ONLY ONE SEX
POSITION I WOULD HAVE TO PUT UP
WITH MY WHOLE LIFE, IT WOULD BE:

THIS IS THE NUMBER OF POSITIONS I LIKE
TO HAVE DURING THE ACT:

DIRTY WORDS

THESE ARE MY TOP DIRTY WORDS:

1.

2.

3.

4.

5.

6.

7.

8.

9.

10.

FILL IN THE BLANKS

THE WORST THING YOU CAN DO DURING
SEX IS TO_____

THE WORST THING YOU CAN SAY DURING
SEX IS_____.

SOME TIME I WOULD LIKE FOR US TO
TRY _____
_____.

I USUALLY_____
AFTER SEX

SEX NOTES

THESE BUDDIES ARE GREAT WHEN YOU FEEL HOT AND WANT TO GET YOUR PARTNER HOT TOO. SIMPLY LEAVE A NOTE IN HIS/HER POCKET, ON THE PILLOW OR THE KITCHEN TABLE AND YOU'LL GET WHAT'S COMING TO YOU. IF YOU WANT TO BE TIED TO THE PLAYGROUND AND WHIPPED WITH A STRAP-ON, JUST SAY IT WITH A NOTE.

DO ME...

- [ ] GROUP SEX
- [ ] MAKE OUT
- [ ] MAKE A PORNO MOVIE
- [ ] DOGGY STYLE
- [ ] 69
- [ ] OUTDOOR SEX
- [ ] DIRTY TALK
- [ ] USING SEX TOYS
- [ ] PHONE SEX
- [ ] ROLE PLAY
- [ ] LET SOMEONE ELSE WATCH US HAVE SEX
- [ ] ACROBATIC SEX POSITIONS
- [ ] BLOW ME/EAT ME
- [ ] STANDING SEX POSITIONS
- [ ] WHIPPING SEX
- [ ] OTHER:

DO ME...

- ☐ GROUP SEX
- ☐ MAKE OUT
- ☐ MAKE A PORNO MOVIE
- ☐ DOGGY STYLE
- ☐ 69
- ☐ OUTDOOR SEX
- ☐ DIRTY TALK
- ☐ USING SEX TOYS
- ☐ PHONE SEX
- ☐ ROLE PLAY
- ☐ LET SOMEONE ELSE WATCH US HAVE SEX
- ☐ ACROBATIC SEX POSITIONS
- ☐ BLOW ME/EAT ME
- ☐ STANDING SEX POSITIONS
- ☐ WHIPPING SEX
- ☐ OTHER:

- ☐ GROUP SEX
- ☐ MAKE OUT
- ☐ MAKE A PORNO MOVIE
- ☐ DOGGY STYLE
- ☐ 69
- ☐ OUTDOOR SEX
- ☐ DIRTY TALK
- ☐ USING SEX TOYS
- ☐ PHONE SEX
- ☐ ROLE PLAY
- ☐ LET SOMEONE ELSE WATCH US HAVE SEX
- ☐ ACROBATIC SEX POSITIONS
- ☐ BLOW ME/EAT ME
- ☐ STANDING SEX POSITIONS
- ☐ WHIPPING SEX
- ☐ OTHER:

DO ME...

- [ ] GROUP SEX
- [ ] MAKE OUT
- [ ] MAKE A PORNO MOVIE
- [ ] DOGGY STYLE
- [ ] 69
- [ ] OUTDOOR SEX
- [ ] DIRTY TALK
- [ ] USING SEX TOYS
- [ ] PHONE SEX
- [ ] ROLE PLAY
- [ ] LET SOMEONE ELSE WATCH US HAVE SEX
- [ ] ACROBATIC SEX POSITIONS
- [ ] BLOW ME/EAT ME
- [ ] STANDING SEX POSITIONS
- [ ] WHIPPING SEX
- [ ] OTHER:

DO ME...

- ☐ GROUP SEX
- ☐ MAKE OUT
- ☐ MAKE A PORNO MOVIE
- ☐ DOGGY STYLE
- ☐ 69
- ☐ OUTDOOR SEX
- ☐ DIRTY TALK
- ☐ USING SEX TOYS
- ☐ PHONE SEX
- ☐ ROLE PLAY
- ☐ LET SOMEONE ELSE WATCH US HAVE SEX
- ☐ ACROBATIC SEX POSITIONS
- ☐ BLOW ME/EAT ME
- ☐ STANDING SEX POSITIONS
- ☐ WHIPPING SEX
- ☐ OTHER:

DO ME...

- ☐ GROUP SEX
- ☐ MAKE OUT
- ☐ MAKE A PORNO MOVIE
- ☐ DOGGY STYLE
- ☐ 69
- ☐ OUTDOOR SEX
- ☐ DIRTY TALK
- ☐ USING SEX TOYS
- ☐ PHONE SEX
- ☐ ROLE PLAY
- ☐ LET SOMEONE ELSE WATCH US HAVE SEX
- ☐ ACROBATIC SEX POSITIONS
- ☐ BLOW ME/EAT ME
- ☐ STANDING SEX POSITIONS
- ☐ WHIPPING SEX
- ☐ OTHER:

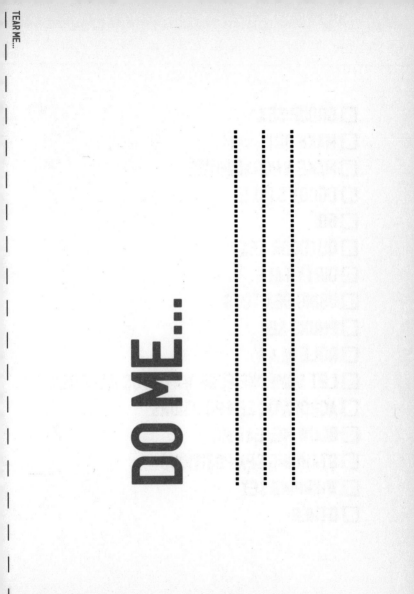

DO ME...

- ☐ GROUP SEX
- ☐ MAKE OUT
- ☐ MAKE A PORNO MOVIE
- ☐ DOGGY STYLE
- ☐ 69
- ☐ OUTDOOR SEX
- ☐ DIRTY TALK
- ☐ USING SEX TOYS
- ☐ PHONE SEX
- ☐ ROLE PLAY
- ☐ LET SOMEONE ELSE WATCH US HAVE SEX
- ☐ ACROBATIC SEX POSITIONS
- ☐ BLOW ME/EAT ME
- ☐ STANDING SEX POSITIONS
- ☐ WHIPPING SEX
- ☐ OTHER:

DO ME...

- [ ] GROUP SEX
- [ ] MAKE OUT
- [ ] MAKE A PORNO MOVIE
- [ ] DOGGY STYLE
- [ ] 69
- [ ] OUTDOOR SEX
- [ ] DIRTY TALK
- [ ] USING SEX TOYS
- [ ] PHONE SEX
- [ ] ROLE PLAY
- [ ] LET SOMEONE ELSE WATCH US HAVE SEX
- [ ] ACROBATIC SEX POSITIONS
- [ ] BLOW ME/EAT ME
- [ ] STANDING SEX POSITIONS
- [ ] WHIPPING SEX
- [ ] OTHER:

DO ME...

- ☐ GROUP SEX
- ☐ MAKE OUT
- ☐ MAKE A PORNO MOVIE
- ☐ DOGGY STYLE
- ☐ 69
- ☐ OUTDOOR SEX
- ☐ DIRTY TALK
- ☐ USING SEX TOYS
- ☐ PHONE SEX
- ☐ ROLE PLAY
- ☐ LET SOMEONE ELSE WATCH US HAVE SEX
- ☐ ACROBATIC SEX POSITIONS
- ☐ BLOW ME/EAT ME
- ☐ STANDING SEX POSITIONS
- ☐ WHIPPING SEX
- ☐ OTHER:

DO ME...

- ☐ GROUP SEX
- ☐ MAKE OUT
- ☐ MAKE A PORNO MOVIE
- ☐ DOGGY STYLE
- ☐ 69
- ☐ OUTDOOR SEX
- ☐ DIRTY TALK
- ☐ USING SEX TOYS
- ☐ PHONE SEX
- ☐ ROLE PLAY
- ☐ LET SOMEONE ELSE WATCH US HAVE SEX
- ☐ ACROBATIC SEX POSITIONS
- ☐ BLOW ME/EAT ME
- ☐ STANDING SEX POSITIONS
- ☐ WHIPPING SEX
- ☐ OTHER:

DO ME...

- ☐ GROUP SEX
- ☐ MAKE OUT
- ☐ MAKE A PORNO MOVIE
- ☐ DOGGY STYLE
- ☐ 69
- ☐ OUTDOOR SEX
- ☐ DIRTY TALK
- ☐ USING SEX TOYS
- ☐ PHONE SEX
- ☐ ROLE PLAY
- ☐ LET SOMEONE ELSE WATCH US HAVE SEX
- ☐ ACROBATIC SEX POSITIONS
- ☐ BLOW ME/EAT ME
- ☐ STANDING SEX POSITIONS
- ☐ WHIPPING SEX
- ☐ OTHER: